# Teaching young children to cook

D1827557

# Teaching young children to cook

Sheila M Baker
Sheila M Thomson

B T Batsford Limited

© Sheila M Baker
and Sheila M Thomson 1973

First published 1974

ISBN 0 7134 2772 8

Designed by Libra Studios
Filmset in 10/12 pt Monophoto Ehrhardt
by Trade Spools, Frome, Somerset
Printed in Great Britain by
The Anchor Press Limited, Tiptree, Essex
and bound by
William Brendon and Son Limited, Tiptree, Essex
for the publishers
B T Batsford Limited
4 Fitzhardinge Street, London W1H 0AH

# Contents

# Approaches to cooking

Introducing cooking into a junior school will always be a popular step. Boys and girls love to eat and they enjoy mixing ingredients. They are at an age before cooking becomes the chore of continuous meal making and they find the whole experience exciting. The aim should be to awaken the pupils' interest and make them eager to learn more.

The approach can be made in several ways:

1 Cooking for the sake of cooking.
2 Cooking to practise weighing and measuring.
3 Cooking to illustrate a project.
4 Cooking to prove an experiment.
5 Cooking to find out what happens if . . .?
6 Cooking to learn cookery terms.

It will not be a structured progressive course such as that used in secondary schools.

**1 Cooking for the sake of cooking** *cf Simple beginnings page 15*
This must be the first consideration when introducing cooking as the children will be longing to eat something themselves or to take something home for the family.

The quickest way for all the children to have this experience is to bake potatoes in their jackets. They will be thrilled to eat these in the playground during a chilly break. Good nutrition thinking might also stem from this. A small cooker will take 12–20 potatoes at a time.

**2 Cooking to practise weighing and measuring** *cf Conversion table page 40*
This exercise is particularly valuable for the younger children who are learning to be accurate. They will be able to see the result if they try rubbing too much fat into the flour. For several years both imperial and metric measurements will be used in connection with foods so a working knowledge of comparisons between them will be useful. Accuracy with handy measures also needs practice.

### 3 Cooking to illustrate a project *cf Sources of reference page 40*

Cooking can often be used to illustrate and support a project which a class or individual pupil is studying, eg

| Canada | wheatlands | bread |
|---|---|---|
| Dairy Farming | milk<br>cheese | drinks, puddings<br>toasted, sauces |
| Fuels | methods of cooking | dampers, girdle scones |
| Special days | Shrove Tuesday | pancakes |
| Transport | travelling | packed meals |

### 4 Cooking to prove an experiment *cf Cooking experiments page 41*

A good deal of science can be taught through food, and very often experiments will seem more valid to the children by using ingredients they know rather than chemicals which are unrecognisable, eg

Effect of heat on cheese
Experiments with yeast and baking powder
Different results from making pastry with different fats
Growing moulds on cultures.

### 5 Cooking to find out what happens if . . .?

Children should be encouraged to have enquiring minds. In cooking, methods and recipes should be challenged. Whilst encouraging children to experiment, teachers must prepare them for the failures which will sometimes happen. This stage in their cooking should, therefore, be deferred until their confidence in their ability to cook has been established:

Will it make any difference to scones if plain or self-raising flour is used?
What would happen if you used equal fat to flour?
half fat to flour?
quarter fat to flour?
Does it ruin a dish to put it into a cold oven?
Can all cakes be made by beating all the ingredients together?

## 6 Cooking to learn cooking terms and skills

These cooking terms and skills have been photographed and are shown in the next section. Some will need to be demonstrated to pupils, but others will only require explanation.

| GETTING READY | | PROCESSES | | CONSISTENCIES | |
|---|---|---|---|---|---|
| 6–8 | weighing and | 19 | sieving (wet) | 47 | pouring |
| | measuring | 21–22 | mashing | 48 | dropping |
| 9 | grating | 23–24 | straining | 49 | soft dough |
| 10 | coring | 25–26 | beating | 50 | stiff dough |
| 11 | pinch of salt | 27 | stirring | 51 | non-sticky dough |
| 12 | greasing | 28 | rubbing-in | | |
| 13–14 | peeling | 29 | kneading (1) | | |
| 15–16 | cutting fresh | 30 | rolling out | | |
| | fruit | 31 | kneading (2) | | |
| 17 | cracking an egg | 32 | whisking | | |
| 18 | separating an | 33–38 | covering a pie | | |
| | egg | 39 | creaming | | |
| 20 | sieving (dry) | 40 | folding | | |
| | | 41 | filling a tin | | |
| | | 42 | filling paper | | |
| | | | cases | | |
| | | 43–44 | glazing | | |
| | | 45–46 | turning pancakes | | |

The numbers refer to the photographs in the next section.

9

# Hygiene

This is most important. Too many cases of food poisoning occur and every child should be trained to handle anything to do with food – ingredients, cloths and utensils – with care. Hands must be washed before starting to cook. Tasting should be encouraged, but so should washing the tasting spoon before returning it to the mixture. Long hair should be tied back to keep it clear of food and also away from flames.

Washing-up will need supervision otherwise tins, particularly, are likely to be put away wet and may become mouldy and rusty. A special bucket or bin should be provided for food waste and should be wrapped securely and emptied into an outside dustbin as soon as possible after cooking. Centrally heated classrooms encourage the growth of bacteria.

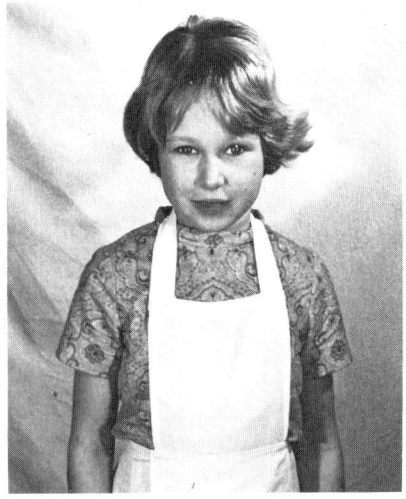

Points which the teacher should instil upon the child:
1   Remember that the food you cook is to be eaten, so keep everything clean.
2   Keep the work table neat and tidy.
3   Do not put utensils or fingers into your mouth and then back into the mixture. Wash them before continuing.
4   Wash dishcloths and tea cloths regularly and hang up to dry after use.

Make yourself neat and tidy by:
1   Combing your hair and tying back if necessary
2   Rolling up long sleeves
3   Washing your hands (don't forget your finger nails)
4   Putting on an apron.

# Safety

Rules applying to safety should be strictly enforced. Potentially dangerous equipment is being used and children should be trained to use it with common sense and respect, eg do not wipe over an electric cooker until the main switch has been turned off; only open the oven door when wearing thick oven gloves. Children should learn the rules about cooking in the same way as they do when learning to ride a bicycle or when handling fireworks.

Many younger children will be frightened of a hot oven. They should be told to stand back as they open the door, so that the first rush of hot air will not hit them full in the face. Suitable oven gloves should give them more confidence when handling hot trays and shelves. Really nervous children could play with the cold oven to get the feel of moving trays and shelves. Train them always to put on oven gloves before opening an oven door.

Whilst some of the techniques taught have fetish qualities, many have evolved which save time and improve the skill of the cook. Which spoon to use for stirring can produce heated arguments but perfectly satisfactory results can be obtained by any type. Metal scratches, gets hot and is noisy, wood will absorb flavours and plastic could melt on the sides of the pan. Children should be taught to select suitable tools and to use them sensibly. They should learn how to cut downwards rather than towards themselves and how to carry knives to avoid accidents.

It will be much safer if a sink with hot water is available in the cooking corner, but it is realised that this is not always possible. If the sink has only a cold tap, the hot water should be carried to it in a large jug or bucket. If the sink is away from the cooking corner a trolley to carry the washing up is useful. This can be used at other times for storing the small equipment.

STEPS ARE A REAL HAZARD

Anything spilt should be wiped up immediately, in case anyone slips on it.

Frying is a potentially dangerous method of cooking and the pupil should be allowed to do so only under strict supervision. As it is likely that young children will be allowed to fry at home we have included omelettes and pancakes so that some of the safety factors can be taught. It can not be too strongly emphasised that children should have a large baking sheet beside them when frying so that should the pan catch fire, it can be covered immediately to exclude the air. A fire blanket should always be near at hand when cooking is in progress. In the event of fire, the main cooker switch should be turned off and the blanket then used, if necessary, to smother the flames.

DEEP FAT FRYING SHOULD NEVER BE ALLOWED

There are some important DO'S and DON'TS to remember when cooking.

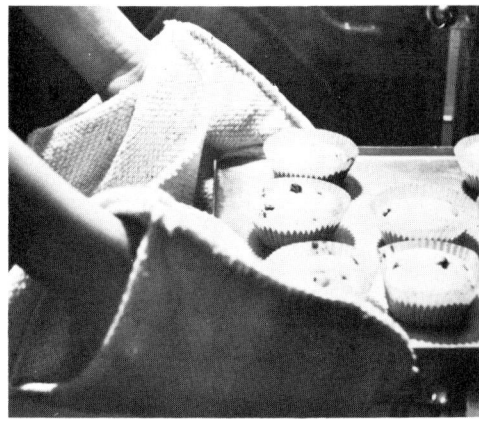

2 Heat can be dangerous. Always use proper oven gloves or an oven cloth when putting food into or taking food out of the oven.

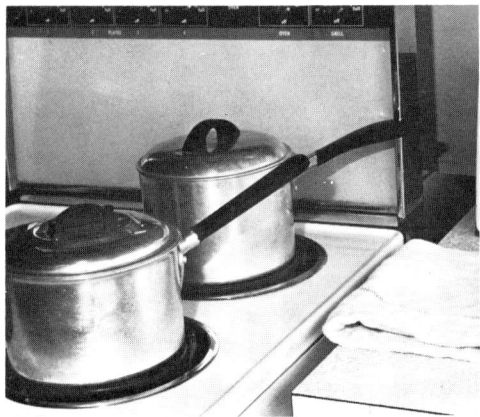

3 Put saucepan handles to the side of the cooker where they cannot be knocked.

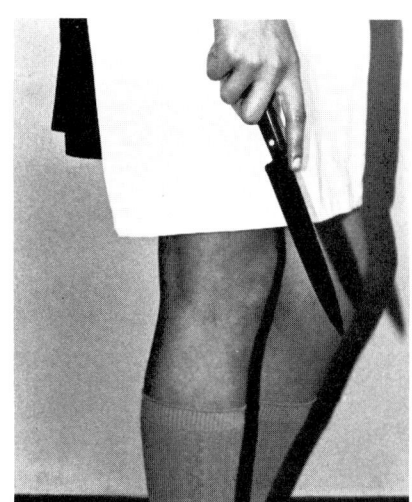

KNIVES NEED TO BE HANDLED
CORRECTLY

4 How to carry

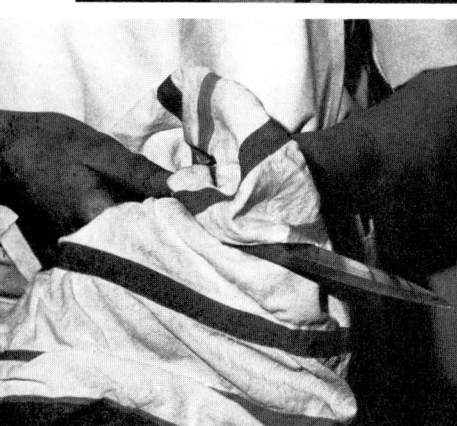

5 How to wipe

# Types and sizes of groups

Cooking can be organised in many different ways:

## 1 Whole class cooking

This is very rarely possible as it is unlikely that space and equipment will be sufficient.
*cf Simple beginnings page 15.*

## 2 Group cooking

(a) as part of a practical option
(b) on a rota basis

These sessions can be organised for a time when a teacher is available, and the size of the groups can vary depending on what is being cooked, eg chocolate crispies only require top heat so numbers need not be so restricted as when oven space is required.

## 3 Individual and small groups

If a cooking corner is established from 1–4 children can use it without direct supervision. The accommodation can then be used more frequently and less advance planning is necessary. Experimental work is more likely to develop under this system.

When the dish being cooked requires eating immediately, eg scrambled egg or cheese pudding, the pupils should be encouraged to lay a table and sit down properly. This can be done quite simply, and is a good opportunity for social training.

If the food is being taken home sampling should be discouraged unless several small things have been made, eg rock cakes. Many pupils will like to share their products, but some control is needed or the vultures will descend. Head teachers will require tact when dealing with pupils who ask them to sample their efforts, if they are not to suffer figure problems.

# Simple beginnings

When cooking is introduced into a school all the pupils will be anxious for a 'turn'. For his/her peace of mind a wise teacher will allow this as soon as possible, starting with simple dishes:

1  **Jacket potatoes**
These require very little preparation and approximately 12–20 can be cooked together in a small oven. They can be slit and eaten with a knob of butter or wedge of cheese.

2  **Baked apples**
In the autumn when apples are plentiful these need not be an expense since only a small amount of filling and sugar for the syrup are a necessary addition. Either an individual or a communal dish may be used.

3  **Chocolate crispies**
As only top heat is required for these a sequence of pupils, depending on the number of saucepans available, can make them. The number need only be limited by the amount of 'drying' space.

4  **Beverages**
Many a good discussion situation can develop round the teapot.

By using these simple dishes it will be possible for all pupils to cook fairly quickly. It will also show them that cooking is not just making cakes.

# Selection of recipes

These may be selected by the teacher and the pupils in a variety of ways:

1 **From any cookery book**
There may be problems if pupils are allowed too free a choice as they may choose recipes that are extravagant or beyond the skills so far acquired.

2 **From a range of books kept in schools**
Recipes could be marked by a starring system to indicate from which ones different groups of pupils may choose. As cooking often involves liquid it is wise to have all recipe books, opened at the appropriate page, inserted into a large polythene bag. Small display stands keep books above the table level and in an easier position for the cook to read.

3 **From large scale posters**
Some of these are available from commercial sources, though the range is limited. Similar posters can be prepared by the teacher, and have the advantage that a group of pupils can work from them at the same time. They do take up rather a large amount of space and storage can be a problem.

4 **From cards**
These can be prepared by the teacher and kept in a filing system or copied by a pupil from the recipe book. In the first case the teacher has complete control over the selection and in the second the pupil must have read through the recipe and method before starting to cook. During cooking they should be slipped into a polythene bag or acetate folder.

5 **Recipes recorded on a cassette**
This system is useful for the non-readers and also means that the teacher can introduce hints and warnings which would be laborious to write and might be skipped by the pupil, eg how to crack an egg. With a simple cassette player with on/off controls and a rewind button, the pupil is in full charge to work at his own pace. A signal, such as a bell, can be introduced on the tape so that the pupil knows when to switch off and carry out those instructions.

**6 Cards and photographs**
These make the pupil almost independent and help to set high standards of work and finish.

Teachers are strongly advised to try out a recipe before using it with children and to check quantities for the size of the tins available.

Always read the instructions provided with the cooker and check the recommended oven temperature with those in the book as they may be different for a very small cooker.

# Providing ingredients

A decision will have to be made on how to provide the ingredients:

**1 From home**
This system makes the teacher very dependent upon the home and the parents' willingness and ability to co-operate. With long journeys, carrying liquids and eggs can be a problem for the pupils. Parents should not be expected to finance cooking for experiment.

**2 From school**
In this case the schools require adequate and suitable storage for perishable foods.

**3 By shopping**
If the school is situated near a suitable shop the pupils could be encouraged to buy the ingredients as part of the cooking experience.

Payment for food will depend on the local authority's system of accounting. It is desirable that experimental work should not require payment from home and that lack of ability to pay should never prevent a pupil from cooking.

# Practical advice

1  It is easier if the pupils can work on formica covered tables, as this surface is suitable for mixing doughs and pastries and for rolling out. If other table surfaces have to be used it will be necessary to provide an oil cloth covering and a pastry board and these should be added to the list of equipment required.

2  It is a wise practice to train the pupils to put all their ingredients out on to plates before beginning to cook. This can act as a check on ingredients both before and after cooking. It will also help to encourage tidy working.

3  We have selected recipes which should cause as few problems as possible with regard to tins and dishes but the following could prove awkward:

Baked apple in too large a dish
Bread if deep sided tin not available
Fruit pie if pie dish too deep for amount of fruit
Fruit pie if no rim for the crust
Omelette if pan too large
Gingerbread – tin size very important

These are the ones to watch if you have to ask pupils to bring dishes from home. Too large a tin presents the biggest problem, because the food will spread too thinly and is liable to burn before it is cooked. Pie dishes without rims are always awkward for pie crusts as it is difficult to prevent them slipping into the filling. A small emergency supply of tins and dishes is always helpful. Foil ones make transport problems easier – returning them should be encouraged.

4  When the recipe requires half an egg the pupils will need to be shown how to divide the beaten egg into two equal sized containers. One egg can then be shared by two pupils.

5  Measuring golden syrup can present problems. There are three fairly simple ways:

(a)  Warm a metal spoon in very hot water and when dry immediately spoon syrup from the tin, so that it runs off the metal easily.
(b)  Sprinkle some of the flour from the recipe on to the scale pan and spoon the syrup on to it. Flour and syrup will then slip easily into the bowl.
(c)  Check the weight of the saucepan on the scales. Then add the syrup using a warmed metal spoon until required weight is reached.

**6**  Creaming margarine will be much easier if it is allowed to soften slightly before use. This can be done by standing the mixing bowl in a bowl of hot water. Cutting the margarine into small pieces will speed the process.

**7**  When the oven is being filled to capacity it should be set 10°C (25°F) higher than the recipe states. Halfway through cooking change the position of the tins.

**8**  Taking food home can be a problem particularly when buses are involved. A large biscuit tin is a good idea as dishes can be carried level and any spills will be contained.

**9**  We have taken 25 g as the equivalent to 1 oz as recommended by the Metrication Board and 500 ml as the equivalent to 1 pt. The tin sizes we have suggested are suitable for the metric recipes. If imperial weights are being used it should be realised that the volume of the finished dish will be proportionally greater.

**10**  Putting mixtures into baking tins is usually done with a spoon and a knife. Young children find this skill difficult to control and need help to prevent the mixture getting up and over the sides of the tins.

**11**  Separating an egg:
**(a)**  The easiest way for young children to manage this is by cracking the whole egg on to a plate. Then cover the yolk with a small cutter or egg cup and pour off the white into a basin.
**(b)**  Alternatively the shell can be cracked in half and the egg white poured off into a basin from the half without a yolk. Then the yolk can be carefully poured into the empty half shell and the remaining white poured into the basin. The yolk may need transferring several times to clear all the white.
**(c)**  An egg separator can be bought.

# Handy measures

THE FOLLOWING HANDY MEASURES EQUAL 25 g

1    level tbs syrup, rice, jam
2    level tbs sultanas, sugar
3    level tbs flour, currants, custard powder
4    level tbs grated cheese
$2\frac{1}{2}$  level tbs icing sugar
5    level tbs fresh breadcrumbs

6 Always stand directly in front of the scales to read them accurately

7 TEASPOONS
level, rounded, heaped

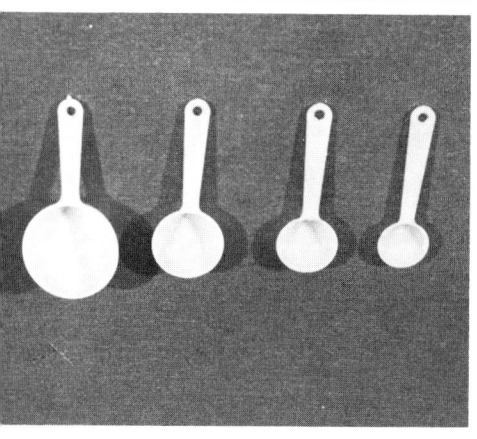

8 STANDARD MEASURING SPOONS
tablespoon, teaspoon, $\frac{1}{2}$ teaspoon, $\frac{1}{4}$ teaspoon

# Glossary

BAKING     cooking in the oven

BINDING     to press a solid and liquid or fat together to form a mass

BLENDING     mixing a powder with liquid to form a paste

BOILING     the liquid in the saucepan should be bubbling gently and not violently

COAT     to cover with a thin layer

CONSISTENCY     thickness of a mixture

DISSOLVE     certain solids, eg sugar and salt, seem to disappear when added to liquids

DOUGH     uncooked mixture

GLAZING     to improve the surface appearance of a cooked dish. There are several ways of doing this and the method selected depends on personal taste

LINING     place greaseproof paper on the inside of cooking tin
ease pastry to fit cooking utensil

MIXING     combining ingredients by continuous stirring

PURÉE     a fine pulp obtained by rubbing cooked food through a sieve

SEAL     close a hole with mixture

SIMMERING     not quite boiling. When the surface of the water is calm, but a slow bubble rises to the surface now and again

SPRINKLE     to scatter a powder evenly by lightly tapping or shaking a spoonful

**Illustrated terms** ►

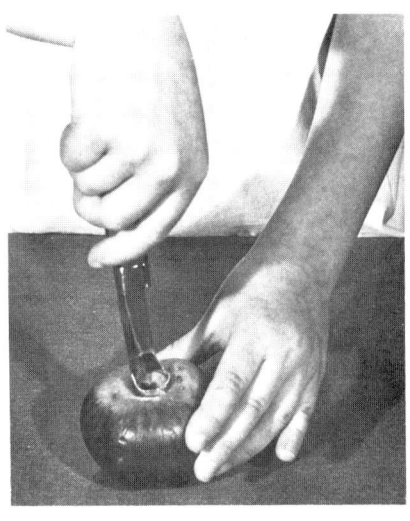

9 GRATING
Hold the grater firmly and press hard as you rub the food up and down

10 CORING
Place the corer carefully and press hard. Two cuts may be necessary

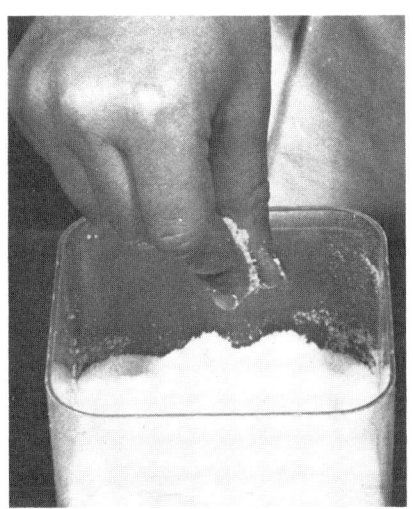

11 PINCH OF SALT
As much as you can hold between your finger and thumb

12 GREASING
Use a small piece of greased paper and rub the surface lightly until smeary all over

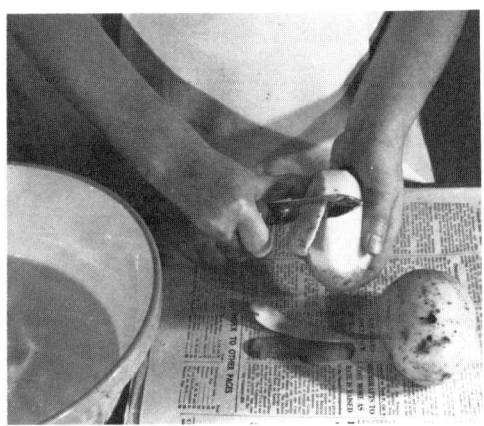

13 PEELING INTO WATER
Suitable for all root vegetables

14 PEELING ONTO PAPER
Suitable for fruit and vegetables

15 CUTTING FRESH ORANGES
Halved and sliced

16 CUTTING FRESH APPLES
Halved, quartered and sliced

17 CRACKING AN EGG
Crack the egg sharply and immediately open the two halves of the egg shell to allow the egg to slip into the basin

18 SEPARATING AN EGG
Crack the egg onto a plate. Place a cutter over the yolk and drain off the white

19 SIEVING (WET)
Rub the solid through the sieve using the back of a wooden spoon

20 SIEVING (DRY)
The powder may be shaken or rubbed through the sieve

**21 MASHING WITH A FORK**
Press the potato against the sides of the saucepan

**22 MASHING WITH A MASHER**
Press downwards

**23 STRAINING VEGETABLES**
Hold the lid slightly back from the saucepan rim and pour carefully

**24 STRAINING MACARONI**
Slowly pour the macaroni and liquid into the sieve. Leave standing until the liquid is in the basin

25 BEATING AN EGG
Use a fork in a circular movement to
mix thoroughly the white and yolk

27 STIRRING
The spoon should cover the bottom of
the saucepan making a figure of eight
as well as circles

26 BEATING A BATTER
Use a wooden spoon to beat air into
the batter

**28 RUBBING-IN**
Rub the thumbs across the fingers
whilst lifting the hands in the bowl

**29 KNEADING RUBBED-IN DOUGHS**
Using the tips of the fingers of the
right hand draw the mixture from
underneath and at the same time keep
the dough turning with the left hand.
Continue until the underside of the
dough is smooth

**30 ROLLING**
Roll directly away from you so that
pressure is on both hands

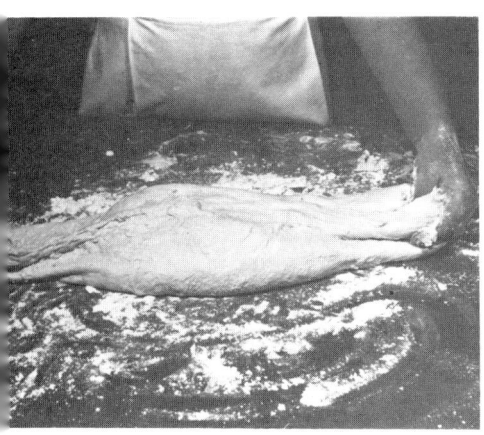

31 KNEADING YEAST DOUGHS
Stretch the dough sideways and then
bring to the middle. Turn a quarter
circle and repeat the process

32 WHISKING
Whisk until stiff

33 Place a pie dish upside down on the pastry and cut round it

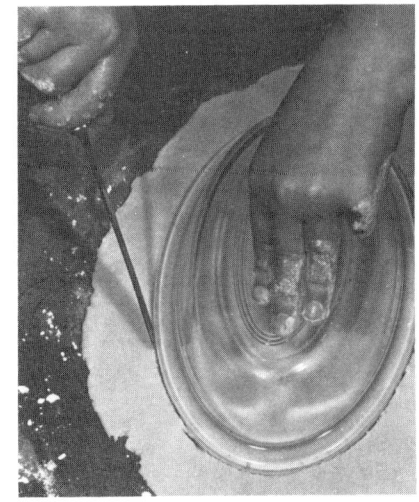

34 Cut strips 2 cm wide to cover the rim of the pie dish

35 Damp the rim and place the strips on it. Do not stretch the pastry

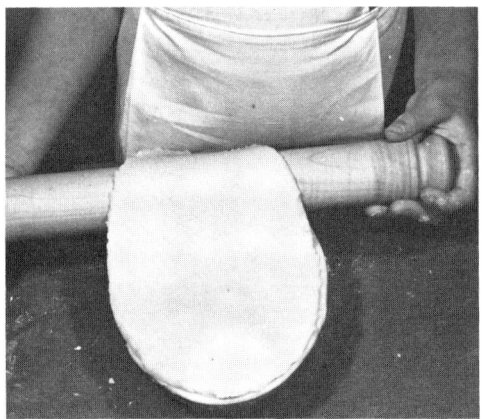

36 Damp the pastry rim and using the rolling pin carefully lift the pastry lid over the pie dish

37 Knock up the edges with the back of a knife

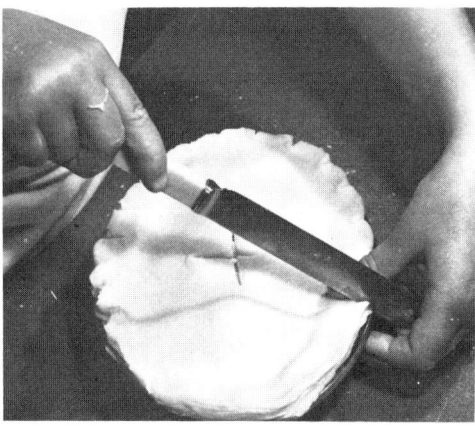

38 Decorate the edge

**39 CREAMING**
First bind the margarine and sugar together using the back of a wooden spoon and then beat using a circular movement

**40 FOLDING**
A very light movement to mix flour and creamed fat gently together

**41 PUTTING MIXTURE INTO A TIN**
Spread the mixture evenly using a round bladed knife. Avoid getting mixture on the sides of the tin

42 PUTTING MIXTURE INTO
PAPER CASES
Take enough mixture on the spoon to
half fill the case and ease off with a
round bladed knife

43 GLAZING PASTRY
Brush the surface with water and then
sprinkle with sugar

44 GLAZING SCONES
Brush the surface with milk

33

45–46 TURNING A PANCAKE
Place the spatula under the half-
cooked pancake and quickly flip over

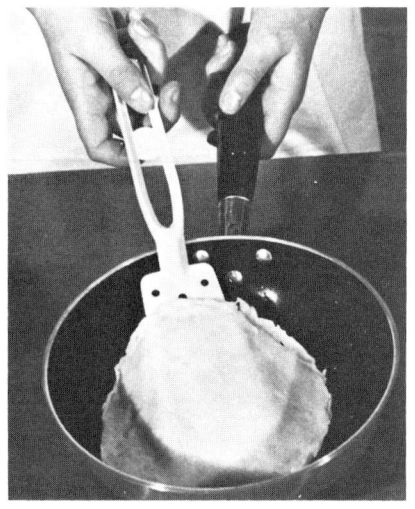

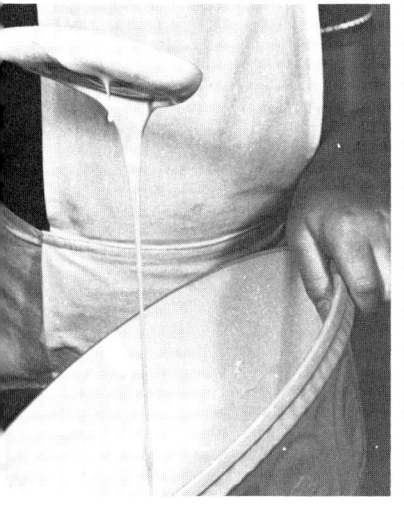

7  Pouring

48  Dropping

Consistencies

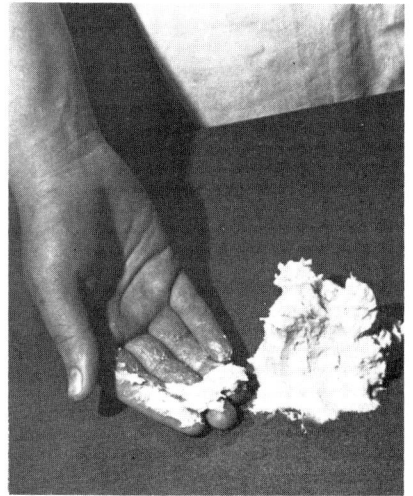

49  Soft dough

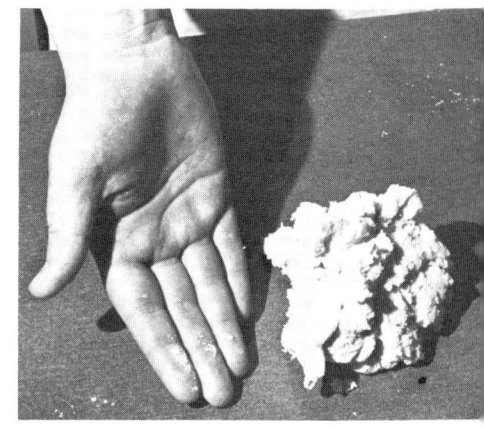

50 Stiff dough

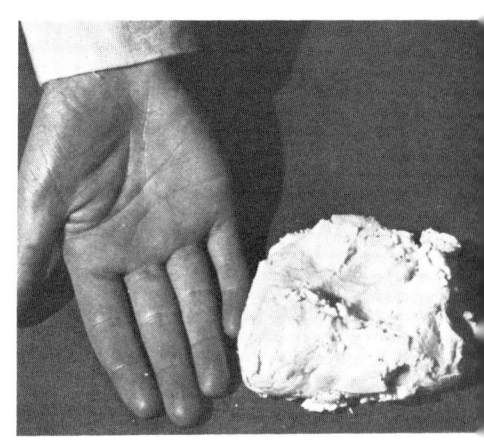

51 Non-sticky dough

# Equipment

Several makes of small cooker which run from 13/15 amp power points are readily available. They can be bought, or hired, from Electricity Boards together with a small cabinet for storage. A trolley to take both cooker and cabinet can be bought.

A firm lightweight folding aluminium table is very useful as a working surface when space is short.

A small refrigerator is necessary if the school is providing the ingredients; these can be hired from Electricity Boards.

A small cupboard with a drawer for cutlery is useful if a large group is cooking.

For ease of reference the small equipment required for the recipes is usually given in the order shown below.

| UTENSILS | CUTLERY | COOKING |
|---|---|---|
| scales | knife: | oven cloth |
| mixing bowl | round bladed | baking sheet |
| basin | vegetable | tins: |
| plate | bread | bread |
| measuring jug | potato peeler | sandwich |
| sieve or strainer | apple corer | bun |
| grater | fork | gingerbread |
| flour dredger | tablespoon | cooling tray |
| egg whisk | dessertspoon | pie dish |
| rolling pin | teaspoon | pie funnel or egg cup |
| chopping board | wooden spoon | mould |
| lemon squeezer | fish slice | oven-proof plate/dish |
| bread board | skewer | saucepan |
| | cutters | panstand |
| | scissors | serving plate |
| | pastry brush | omelette pan |
| | spatula | frying pan |
| | | paper cases |
| | | pudding basin |

The above equipment will be required if all the recipes in this book are to be tried. The quantities required will depend on the number of pupils cooking at one time.

When buying the equipment there are several points to note:

(a) Check that the scales' dial can easily be read by young children
(b) Check that the baking tins will fit the oven to be used
(c) Avoid small 'toy' equipment which is not easy to use and is often fragile

ADDITIONAL EQUIPMENT

| | | |
|---|---|---|
| washing-up bowl | draining rack OR mat | hand towel |
| mop or sponge | teacloth | bar soap |
| dish cloth | detergent | refuse bucket |

# Abbreviations

| | | |
|---|---|---|
| tsp: teaspoon | lb: pound | cm: centimetres |
| tbs: tablespoon | pt: pint | F: Fahrenheit |
| g: gram(s) | ml: millilitres | C: Centigrade or Celsius |
| oz: ounce | mm: millimetres | |

# Equipment

Collect all the equipment before
starting to cook

# Sources of reference

Details of teaching aids in connection with food, both free and those available for purchase, are given in the July numbers of *Housecraft*, the magazine published by the Association of Teachers of Domestic Science, Hamilton House, Mabledon Place, London WC1H 9BB, and *Home Economics* published by Forbes Publications Ltd, Hartree House, Queensway, London W2 4SH. Copies of these will probably be available in the larger teachers' centres.

# Conversion tables

| Gas mark | Centigrade | Fahrenheit | Heat of oven |
|---|---|---|---|
| Below thermostat setting | °C | °F | |
| | 100 | 200 | Very cool |
| $\frac{1}{4}$ | 110 | 225 | Very cool |
| $\frac{1}{2}$ | 130 | 250 | Very cool |
| 1 | 140 | 275 | Very cool |
| 2 | 150 | 300 | Cool |
| 3 | 160 | 325 | Warm |
| 4 | 180 | 350 | Moderate |
| 5 | 190 | 375 | Fairly hot |
| 6 | 200 | 400 | Fairly hot |
| 7 | 220 | 425 | Hot |
| 8 | 230 | 450 | Very hot |
| 9 | 240 | 475 | Very hot |

EXACT CONVERSIONS IMPERIAL TO METRIC

| WEIGHTS | LIQUIDS | MEASUREMENTS |
|---|---|---|
| 1 oz = 28·35 g | $\frac{1}{4}$ pt = 142 ml | 1 in. = 2.54 cm |
| 2 oz = 56·70 g | $\frac{1}{2}$ pt = 284 ml | 6 in. = 15·20 cm |
| 4 oz = 113·40 g | 1 pt = 568 ml | $\frac{1}{8}$ in. = 3 mm |
| 8 oz = 226·80 g | | |

# Cooking experiments

### 1 Conduction

saucepan     metal tablespoon     plastic spoon
panstand     wooden spoon

Half fill a small saucepan with boiling water. Stand in it a metal tablespoon, a wooden spoon and a plastic spoon. After 5 minutes feel the handle of each spoon. Which spoon would you prefer to use for stirring a hot saucepan?

### 2 Boiling liquids

125 ml water     2 small saucepans
125 ml milk     panstand

Put 125 ml of water into one small saucepan and 125 ml of milk into a similar sized saucepan. Bring both slowly to the boil watching all the time. Which one should you not turn your back on when it is on the cooker? Now make a milk drink.

### 3 Hygiene

10 petri dishes OR 10 paste pots and lids     250 ml water
*Agar* OR 2 pkts gelatine     1 *Oxo* cube OR stock cube

1   Make up *Agar* or dissolve gelatine and *Oxo* in water.
2   Pour into petri dishes, cover and leave until set.
3   Label one dish control and leave unopened.
4   Open each dish in turn and on surface of

    (a)   put a hair        (f)   rub a sucked finger
    (b)   rub a dish cloth    (g)   rub a clean finger
    (c)   rub a tea cloth     (h)   cough into dish
    (d)   rub a dirty finger   (i)   rub a used hanky
    (e)   rub a fork that has been dropped on the floor

All dishes should be covered immediately. Leave in a warm place for about a week and then open and note any growth.

NOTE:   If petri dishes are used progress can be watched through the glass top.

## 4   Tea

| kettle | 2 cups | milk |
|---|---|---|
| 2 small teapots | | 2 tea bags |

1   Put 2 pts cold water into the kettle making certain the element is covered.

2   Collect 2 similar sized small teapots and put 1 teabag into each pot.

3   When the kettle is boiling pour 1 pint of water into one teapot.

4   Let the kettle stand for 1 minute and then pour the remaining water into the second teapot. Leave both teapots to stand.

5   Meantime collect two cups and after 5 minutes pour out a cup from each pot. Compare the colour and flavour of each. Is boiling water necessary for good tea? Add milk to the cup you would prefer to drink.


## 5   Baking powder

| $\frac{1}{2}$ tsp baking powder | test tube |
|---|---|
| 1 tsp bicarbonate of soda | test tube holder |
| 1 tsp cream of tartar | saucepan |
| 125 ml ice cold water | panstand |
| 125 ml hot water | |

Baking powder gives off a gas when it is mixed with moisture and heated. Put $\frac{1}{2}$ tsp baking powder at the bottom of test tube and pour in ice cold water to half fill the tube. Shake and note reaction.

Stand the test tube in a saucepan of water and heat it.

Evidence of gas is shown by the effervescence.

Repeat the experiment using hot water instead of the ice cold water.

(a)   What happened when the ice cold water was poured into the test tube? Did heating make any difference?

(b)   What happened when the hot water was poured on to the baking powder?

(c)   Taste the remaining liquid.

REPEAT THE EXPERIMENT WITH

1   $\frac{1}{2}$ tsp bicarbonate of soda.

2   $\frac{1}{2}$ tsp cream of tartar.

3   $\frac{1}{2}$ tsp bicarbonate of soda and $\frac{1}{2}$ tsp cream of tartar.

## 6   Yeast

| | | |
|---|---|---|
| 30 g yeast | 4 tbs hot water | test tube holder |
| 1 tsp sugar | 1 tsp salt | saucepan |
| 2 tbs warm water | ice cubes | panstand |
| 2 tbs ice cold water | 5 test tubes | |

To discover the conditions necessary for the growth of yeast.

Cream 25 g yeast and 1 tsp sugar together and divide between 4 test tubes:

(a)   Add warm water and keep warm

(b)   Add 1 tsp salt and keep warm

(c)   Add iced water and put in refrigerator or stand in a basin of ice cubes
      Ice cubes can be brought from home in a thermos flask

(d)   Add hot water. Stand in a saucepan of hot water and bring to boil. Boil for
15 minutes

Into a fifth test tube (e) put 5 g yeast and warm water and keep warm.
After 1 hour stand (c) in warm water. What happens?

NOTE:   Warm = blood heat, ie should feel slightly warm to the finger.


## 7   Moulds

| | | |
|---|---|---|
| 2 cubes of white bread | 2 jam jars | microscope |
| 2 saucers | | magnifying glass |

1   Cut 2 small cubes of white bread and soak one in water.

2   Put each cube on to a saucer and leave for $\frac{1}{2}$ an hour.

3   Then cover with a jam jar and leave for several days.

Note which cube develops mould. Examine the mould with a magnifying glass
and under a microscope.

If the school has access to a refrigerator two additional cubes – one damp, one
dry – can be placed in it for comparison.

## 8 Sugar

SUGARS

| | | | |
|---|---|---|---|
| granulated | soft brown | icing | teaspoon |
| castor | cube | | paper towel |
| demerara | coffee | | |

Collect as many different examples of sugar as possible and examine the crystals under a microscope.

1 Stick out your tongue and wipe it dry with a paper towel.

2 Then get a friend to sprinkle a few granulated sugar grains on to your tongue with a teaspoon. Can you taste it?

3 Put your tongue back into your mouth and dissolve the sugar with your saliva. Can you taste the sugar now?

Food can only be tasted when it has been dissolved.

## 9 Flour

| | | |
|---|---|---|
| 25 g flour | muslin | baking sheet |
| cold water | string | |
| few drops iodine | basin | |

To show that flour consists of starch and gluten.

1 Mix 25 g flour to a dough with a little cold water.

2 Put the lump of dough in the middle of a 25 cm square of muslin. Gather the edges together and tie to make a bag.

3 Squeeze the bag in a basin of cold water until the water becomes milky. Add a few drops of iodine, which should turn the mixture black, proving that starch is present.

4 Continue working the flour mixture under the cold tap until the water runs clear.

5 Untie the bag to examine the remaining substance, which is gluten.

6 Bake a small ball of gluten in the oven. It will expand.

This property of gluten is involved whenever you cook anything that will rise. It is the gluten which is stretched by the gas given off by the raising agent or the air that is incorporated during the mixing, which expands on heating, eg bread, cakes. Baking solidifies the gluton to form the structure of the baked product.

## 10  Starch

1 tsp cornflour        2 small jam jars        few drops of iodine
2 tsp cold water       teaspoon

To show that saliva digests starch and turns it into sugar.

Take 2 small jam jars and put ½ tsp cornflour into each.

**Jar (a)**  Mix cornflour to a paste with 2 tsp cold water. Test with iodine to prove that starch is present.

**Jar (b)**  Mix cornflour to a paste with a little saliva. Leave for 10 minutes. Add 1 drop of iodine and the mixture will turn a reddish-yellow colour showing that the starch has been turned into sugar.

## 11  Cereals

1

3 tsp cornflour        basin
1 tsp arrowroot        3 small saucepans
500 ml water

1  Put 1 teaspoon cornflour into a basin and mix to a smooth paste with 125 ml of water. Leave to stand for 1 hour.

2  Put 1 teaspoon of cornflour into a small saucepan and add 125 ml water. Bring to the boil and observe the result.

3  Put 1 teaspoon of cornflour into a small saucepan and mix to a smooth paste with 125 ml of cold water. Bring to the boil stirring all the time with a wooden spoon.

Compare the results of 3 with 2.

Would you use methods 1, 2 or 3 for making cornflour mould?

4  Put 1 teaspoon of arrowroot into a small saucepan and mix to a smooth paste with 125 ml of cold water. Bring to the boil stirring all the time.

Compare your result with the cornflour mixture.

2

25 g rice, sago, tapioca, pearl barley, oatmeal, cornflour and arrowroot
1750 ml water                              saucepans

1  Put 25 g rice into a saucepan, add 250 ml water and bring to boil and stir all the time.

2  Simmer until mixture thickens or the grains soften.

Repeat experiment with the other cereals.

NOTE

1  Any change while mixture comes to boil.

2  How long the mixture must simmer before it thickens or the grain softens.

NOTE:  Cornflour and arrowroot must be stirred all the time.

## 12 Cheese

| 75 g cheddar cheese | teaspoon | saucepan |
| 2 tbs milk | knife | panstand |
| | grater | baking sheet |

To find the effect of heat on cheese

1  Heat a slice of cheese in a saucepan.
2  Grate 25 g cheese and mix with 1 tsp milk and heat in a saucepan.
3  Heat a slice of cheese on a baking sheet under the grill.
4  Grate 25 g cheese and mix with 1 tsp milk and heat on a baking sheet under the grill.

The results can be eaten; what difference is there in flavour and texture between the sliced and grated samples?
   Make soft cheese with sour milk and compare with cheddar cheese.
   Serve with bread or biscuits.


## 13 Fats

| 1 slice of white bread | bread board and knife |
| 10 g butter | round-bladed knife |
| 10 g soft margarine | 3 saucers |
| 10 g hard margarine | |

1  Toast a slice of white bread on both sides and cut into 3 fingers.
2  Put 10 g butter, hard margarine and soft margarine on to 3 saucers.
3  With a round-bladed knife spread each fat on to a different finger of toast. Which spreads most easily?
4  Now eat the finger of toast. Which do you prefer?
5  Compare the smell, colour and texture of each fat.
6  Now label the saucers A, B and C and conduct a consumer test among your friends to find out which they prefer.
7  Prepare a graph of the results.

Compare the prices of butter, hard and soft margarine.

## 14 Short crust pastry

| | | | |
|---|---|---|---|
| 25 g margarine | 2–3 tbs cold water | small basin | rolling pin |
| pinch salt | scales | plate | round-bladed knife |
| 50 g plain flour | mixing bowl | flour dredger | tablespoon |
| | | | teaspoon |

To compare pastry made with different fats.

Suggested alternative fats: lard, equal amounts of margarine and lard, butter, cooking fat, dripping.

METHOD
1  Rub the dry ingredients together.
2  Mix to a dry dough with the cold water.
3  Roll out 3 mm ($\frac{1}{8}$ in.) thick and bake on a baking sheet for 10–15 minutes 220°C (425°F) or Gas mark 7.

NOTE: The same temperature oven, shelf and cooking time should be used for all samples.

COMPARE THE RESULTS:
1  Which fat rubbed in most easily?     3  Taste.
2  The texture of the cooked pastries.   4  Appearance.


## 15 Proportions for pastry dough

| | | | |
|---|---|---|---|
| 70 g margarine | 8–12 tsps cold water | small basin | rolling pin |
| pinch salt | scales | plate | round-bladed knife |
| 200 g plain flour | mixing bowl | flour dredger | tablespoon |
| | | | teaspoon |

To compare the amounts of fat in pastry.

RECIPES
1  50 g plain flour, pinch of salt, and water to make a dry dough.
2  50 g plain flour, pinch of salt, 10 g fat, and water to make a dry dough.
3  50 g plain flour, pinch of salt, 25 g fat, and water to make a dry dough.
4  50 g plain flour, pinch of salt, 35 g fat, and water to make a dry dough.

METHOD     MAKE UP EACH RECIPE IN TURN BY:
1  Rubbing the dry ingredients together.
2  Mixing to a dry dough with the cold water.
3  Rolling out 3 mm thick and baking on a baking sheet for 10–15 minutes. Gas mark 7. Electric 220°C (425°F).

COMPARE THE RESULTS:
1  Ease of rubbing in and kneading.    3  Taste.
2  Shortness of cooked pastry.          4  Appearance.

**Finished dishes**

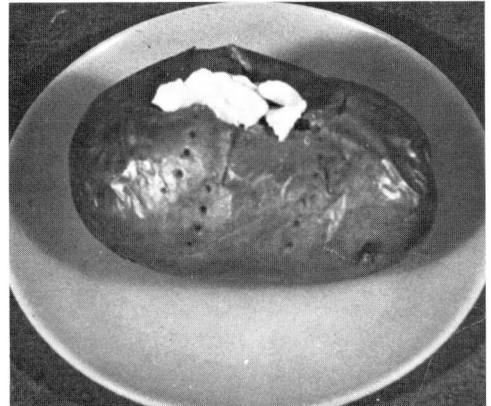

Jacket potatoes

Baked cheese potatoes

Cheese and potato pie

Milk drink and Sandwiches

Scrambled egg

Bread and butter pudding

Chocolate crispies

Rice pudding

Milk mould

Welsh rarebit

Cheese pudding

Macaroni cheese

Baked apple

Apple crumble

Fruit fool

Tea bread

White bread

Bread rolls

Melting moments

Jam buns

Rock cakes

Victoria sandwich

Queen cakes

Scones

Christmas pudding

Queen of puddings

Fresh fruit salad

Open tart

Fruit pie

Omelette

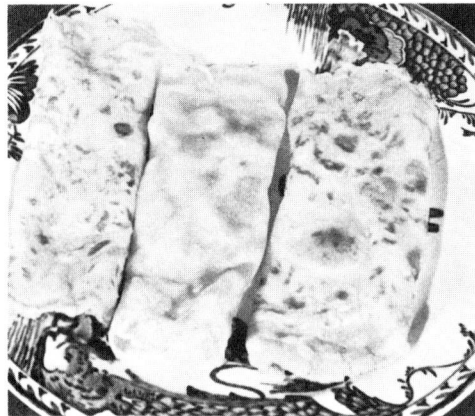

Pancakes

Gingerbread

Peppermint creams

# Recipe analysis

The recipes have been selected to cover basic skills and methods. They are suggestions only and are not intended as a complete scheme of work. The order shown is progressive and in many cases relies on previous experience.

| | |
|---|---|
| 1   Jacket potatoes | using the cooker |
| 2   Chocolate crispies | weighing and measuring |
| 3   Milk drink | boiling milk |
| 4   Baked cheese potatoes | grating |
| 5   Baked apple | coring |
| 6   Cheese and potato pie | peeling and mashing, simmering |
| 7   Rice pudding | greasing |
| 8   Welsh rarebit | using the grill |
| 9   Scrambled egg | cracking an egg, stirring |
| 10   Bread and butter pudding | cutting bread and butter |
| 11   Sandwiches | suitable fillings |
| 12   Christmas pudding | steaming |
| 13   Fruit crumble | rubbing-in |
| 14   Melting moment biscuits | non-sticky consistency |
| 15   Milk mould | blending method |
| 16   Cheese pudding | separating an egg |
| 17   Fruit fool | sieving |
| 18   Macaroni cheese | roux method |
| 19   Tea bread | dropping consistency |
| 20   Yeast dough | using yeast |
| (a)   White bread | kneading dough |
| (b)   Bread rolls | shaping dough |
| 21   Queen of puddings | meringue |
| 22   Jam buns | kneading lightly |
| 23   Rock cakes | stiff dough |
| 24   Fresh fruit salad | cutting fresh fruit, boiling syrup |
| 25   Victoria sandwich | |
| (a)   One stage method | quick method |
| (b)   Traditional method | creaming, folding |
| 26   Queen cakes | filling paper cases |
| 27   Gingerbread | melting method |
| 28   Scones | soft dough consistency |
| 29   Short crust pastry | rolling |
| (a)   Open tart | decorating edge |

|     | **(b) Fruit pie** | covering a pie dish |
| 30  | **Omelette** | frying |
| 31  | **Pancakes** | batter |
| 32  | **Peppermint creams** | uncooked sweets |

NOTE

1 An asterisk means that the pupils should ask the teacher to check or watch the stage that has been reached.

2 A number in brackets refers to the photograph illustrating that part.

3 When measuring, all spoonfuls should be level unless otherwise stated.

4 It is good practice to train the pupils to collect all the equipment required before starting to cook. Then the use of any unfamiliar piece of equipment can be explained to them.

# Recipes 1-32

## Jacket potatoes

1 old potato     knob of margarine

THE FOLLOWING ARE ALSO NEEDED
paper towel    knife      oven cloth
                fork       cooling tray
                skewer

OVEN TEMPERATURE
Gas mark 6. Electric 200°C (400°F)

METHOD
1 Wash the potato and dry it with the paper towel.
2 Prick it in 6 places with the fork.
3* Using the oven cloth place the potato on to the oven shelf.
4* Bake until soft. Test with the skewer after 1 hour. When cooked it will be soft in the middle.
5 Take the potato from the oven using the oven cloth and place on the cooling tray.
6 Cut a cross on the top of the potato and put a knob of margarine in the hole.

The potato may be rubbed with a greasy paper before cooking to make the skin softer when cooked.

## Chocolate crispies *(9 cakes)*

| | |
|---|---|
| 25 g (1 oz) margarine | 1 tbs golden syrup |
| 25 g (1 oz) sugar | 40 g (1½ oz) cornflakes |
| 25 g (1 oz) cocoa | |

THE FOLLOWING ARE ALSO NEEDED

| | | | |
|---|---|---|---|
| scales | knife – round bladed | baking sheet | serving plate |
| plate | metal tablespoon | saucepan | 9 paper cases |
| | wooden spoon | panstand | |

METHOD

1   Tip the cornflakes on to the plate.

2   Put the margarine, sugar, cocoa and golden syrup into the saucepan.

3*  Warm the saucepan and melt the ingredients slowly stirring all the time. Take care they do not boil.

4*  Remove the saucepan from the heat and leave to cool slightly.

5   Lay the paper cases on the baking sheet.

6*  Add the cornflakes to the saucepan and stir (27) lightly with the metal tablespoon until the cornflakes are coated with the chocolate mixture.

7   Using the spoon and the knife carefully (42) put the mixture into the paper cases.

8   Leave to set.


## Milk drink *(flavoured)*

1 cup milk

1–2 level tsp flavouring – coffee or chocolate according to taste, sugar to taste

THE FOLLOWING ARE ALSO NEEDED

cup and saucer OR     milk saucepan     teaspoon
mug with handle

METHOD

1   Measure the milk.

2   Pour the milk into the saucepan.

3   Put flavouring and sugar, if required, into the cup and stir in a little of the cold milk.

4   Heat the milk. Watch it all the time.

5*  Pour the milk into the cup.

6   Fill the saucepan with cold water and leave until you are ready to wash up.

If there are instructions on the tin you are using, follow them.

## Baked cheese potato

| | |
|---|---|
| 1 large potato | pinch of salt |
| 25 g (1 oz) hard cheese | shake of pepper |

THE FOLLOWING ARE ALSO NEEDED

| | | |
|---|---|---|
| scales | knife | oven cloth |
| basin | fork | baking sheet |
| plate | tablespoon | cooling tray |
| grater | skewer | |
| paper towel | | |

OVEN TEMPERATURE

Gas mark 6. Electric 200°C (400°F)

METHOD

1   Wash the potato and dry it with the paper towel.

2   Prick it in 6 places with the fork.

3*  Using the oven cloth place the potato on the oven shelf.

4*  Bake until soft. Test with the skewer after 1 hour. When cooked it will be soft in the middle.

5   Take the potato from the oven using the oven cloth (2) and place on the cooling tray.

6   Grate (9) the cheese on to the plate.

7   Cut the potato in half lengthwise.

8*  Using the tablespoon scoop out the middle of the potato into the basin. Be careful not to break the skin.

9*  Mash (21) the potato pulp with the fork until no lumps are left.

10  Add the grated cheese, salt and pepper and mix together with the fork.

11  Using the tablespoon and the knife put this mixture into the potato skins. Pile it up in the middle.

12  Smooth the top with the fork.

13* Stand the potato cases on the baking sheet.

14  Return to the oven for 20 minutes. The cheese will melt and the top will brown.

## Baked apple

| 1 large cooking apple | 1 tbs sultanas | |
|---|---|---|
| 1 tbs brown sugar | 1 tbs golden syrup | water |

THE FOLLOWING ARE ALSO NEEDED

| scales | vegetable knife | oven cloth |
|---|---|---|
| plate | apple corer | baking sheet |
| measuring jug | tablespoon | oven-proof dish |
| paper towel | teaspoon | (just larger than the apple) |
| | skewer | |

OVEN TEMPERATURE
Gas mark 4. Electric 180°C (350°F)

METHOD

1   Wash the apple and dry it with the paper towel.
2*   Take out the core carefully using apple corer (10) or potato peeler.
3*   Using the point of the vegetable knife make a slit round the middle of the apple, only just cutting the skin, making sure that you meet at the beginning.
4   Put the apple into the dish.
5   Fill the middle with the sultanas.
6*   Spoon the golden syrup straight from the tin over the top of the apple.
7   Sprinkle the brown sugar over the syrup.
8   Using the teaspoon sprinkle a little water over the sugar to help form a toffee mixture.
9   Pour the rest of the water carefully into the dish.
10*   Place the dish on the baking sheet and put in the oven.
11   Bake for approximately 1 hour – the top half of the apple skin will rise and the apple flesh becomes fluffy.
12*   Test the apple with the skewer. It should be soft in the middle.

DIFFERENT FILLINGS: 1 tbs mincemeat, 1 tbs bramble jelly, 1 tbs other dried fruits (raisins, candied peel etc) OR 1 tbs brown sugar and knob of butter.

# Cheese and potato pie

| | |
|---|---|
| 400 g (1 lb) potatoes | 25 g (1 oz) margarine |
| 1 tsp salt | 2 tbs milk |
| 50 g (2 oz) hard cheese | shake of pepper |

THE FOLLOWING ARE ALSO NEEDED

| | | |
|---|---|---|
| scales | vegetable knife | oven cloth |
| plate | potato peeler | saucepan |
| grater | fork | panstand |
| chopping board | teaspoon | pie dish |
| | skewer | |

OVEN TEMPERATURE
Gas mark 6. Electric 200°C (400°F)

METHOD

1   Wash and peel (13–14) the potatoes. Cut into even-sized pieces.

2   Put the potatoes into the saucepan and cover with cold water. Add the salt.

3*   Bring the potatoes to the boil, turn heat to low and simmer for about 20 minutes. When cooked the potatoes will be soft. Test with the skewer.

4   While potatoes are cooking grate (9) the cheese onto the plate.

5*   Carefully strain (23) the potato water into the sink.

6*   When the potatoes are dry, mash (21) with the fork making sure no lumps are left.

7   Add the margarine, pepper, milk and ¾ of the grated cheese. Mix thoroughly.

8*   Put the mixture into the pie dish, smoothing the top with the fork.

9   Sprinkle the rest of the cheese on top.

10*   Bake for 20 minutes until golden brown on top and the mixture is thoroughly heated.

## Rice pudding

250 ml (½ pt) milk       knob of margarine
25 g (1 oz) rice         grated nutmeg
1 tbs sugar

THE FOLLOWING ARE ALSO NEEDED
scales           tablespoon      oven cloth
measuring jug    teaspoon        baking sheet
strainer                         pie dish

OVEN TEMPERATURE
Gas mark 2. Electric 150°C (300°F)

METHOD
1  Grease (12) the pie dish with a margarine paper.
2  Wash the rice in the strainer by running water through it.
3  Put the rice and the sugar into the pie dish.
4  Carefully pour the milk into the pie dish.
5* Cut the knob of margarine into small pieces and float on top of the milk.
Sprinkle the nutmeg over the pudding using the teaspoon.
6  Place the pie dish on the baking sheet and put in the oven.
7  Bake for 1½ hours until the pudding is brown on top and creamy underneath.

If cooking time is limited, heat the milk and rice in a saucepan for 5 minutes before putting into the pie dish, then cook for about 1 hour.

## Welsh rarebit

| 25 g (1 oz) hard cheese | shake of pepper | 2 tsp milk |
| 15 g (½ oz) butter | pinch of salt | |
| 1 slice bread | pinch of mustard (optional) | |

THE FOLLOWING ARE ALSO NEEDED

| scales | plate | knife (round bladed) | wooden spoon |
| basin | grater | teaspoon | serving plate |

METHOD

1 Grate (9) the cheese finely.

2 Mix milk, grated cheese, salt, pepper, and mustard if used, in the small basin until a paste is formed.

3 Light the grill and put the serving plate to warm.

4 Toast the bread on both sides under the grill.

5* Put the toast on the cooking plate and butter one side. Spread with the cheese paste, right to the edges.

6 Put the toast back under the grill and cook until the cheese is light brown and crisp on top.

7 Place on the warm serving plate and eat at once.


## Scrambled egg on toast

| 25 g (1 oz) butter | 1 tbs milk | pinch of salt |
| 1 slice of bread | 1 egg | shake of pepper |

THE FOLLOWING ARE ALSO NEEDED

| scales | knife | tablespoon | panstand |
| basin | fork | wooden spoon | |
| plate | | small saucepan | |

METHOD

1 Crack (17) the egg shell and carefully drop the egg into the basin and add salt, pepper and milk.

2 Beat (25) with the fork until frothy.

3 Light the grill and put the serving plate to warm.

4 Toast the bread on both sides until a golden brown. Keep it warm on the serving plate.

5 Put a knob of butter the size of a hazel nut into the saucepan and heat until melted.

6* Pour the egg mixture into the saucepan and cook over a low heat, stirring (27) all the time, until the mixture sets.

7 Butter the toast, pile the egg mixture on top and eat at once.

## Bread and butter pudding

| 250 ml ($\frac{1}{2}$ pt) milk | 3 slices bread | 1 tbs sugar |
| 25 g (1 oz) butter | 1 egg | 1 tbs currants |

THE FOLLOWING ARE ALSO NEEDED

| scales | knife | oven cloth | pie dish |
| basin | fork | baking sheet | |
| plate | tablespoon | saucepan | |
| measuring jug | skewer | panstand | |

OVEN TEMPERATURE
Gas mark3. Electric 160°C (325°F)

METHOD

1   Grease (12) the pie dish.

2   Butter the bread and cut each slice into 4 strips.

3*  Cover the bottom of the pie dish with strips of bread and butter.

4   Sprinkle with the currants.

5   Cover the currants with the rest of the bread and butter strips.

6   Crack (17) the egg shell and carefully drop the egg into the basin, and then beat (25) with the fork until frothy.

7   Stir the sugar into the egg.

8*  Heat the milk until nearly boiling and pour on to the egg, stirring all the time.

9   Carefully pour the egg mixture over the bread and butter and stand for 5 minutes.

10  Place the pie dish on to the baking sheet and put into the oven.

11  Bake for about 45 minutes until golden brown on top and set – test this by putting a skewer into the middle of the pudding – if cooked there will be no runny mixture.

## Egg sandwiches

| | | |
|---|---|---|
| 4 slices bread | 1 tsp salad cream | pinch salt |
| Butter for spreading | 1 egg | shake of pepper |

THE FOLLOWING ARE ALSO NEEDED

| | | |
|---|---|---|
| basin | knife (round bladed) | small saucepan |
| plate | fork | panstand |
| bread board | teaspoon | |
| | breadknife | |

METHOD

1 Put the egg into a small saucepan and just cover with cold water.

2 Put the saucepan on the cooker and bring the water to the boil. Lower the heat so that the water is simmering and cook the egg for 10 minutes to hard boil it.

3* Spread the bread with softened butter evenly and into each corner.

4* Place the saucepan in the sink and run cold water into it to replace the boiling water. Leave the egg to cool.

5 Remove the shell from the cold egg and put the egg into the basin.

6 Cut the egg into small pieces with the knife and then mash together the white and yolk using the fork.

7 Add salt, pepper and salad cream and mix together thoroughly.

8* Place the egg mixture on 2 of the slices of bread and spread evenly.

9 Cover the filling with the remaining slices and press gently together.

10 The crusts may be cut from the bread, or left on according to the occasion for which they are needed.

11 The sandwiches may be cut into quarters, triangles or fingers.

VARIATIONS

**Cheese:**
slices
grated and made into paste with butter
spread
**Ham:** slices
**Sardine:** mashed with salt and pepper
**Tomato:** sliced with salt and pepper
**Banana:** mashed – these are very tasty if made with brown bread
**Marmite and cucumber:** marmite spread thinly with sliced cucumber on top

Lettuce, cress and watercress can be added to many of these fillings.

## Christmas pudding

75 g (3 oz) flour
25 g (1 oz) white
  breadcrumbs
50 g (2 oz) suet
300 g (12 oz) dried fruit

40 g (1½ oz) brown sugar
60 ml (⅛ pt) milk
1 orange
1 apple

1 egg
½ tsp mixed spice
¼ tsp gravy browning

THE FOLLOWING ARE ALSO NEEDED

scales
mixing bowl
basin
plate
measuring jug
grater
chopping board

lemon squeezer
paper towel
vegetable knife
potato peeler
fork
tablespoon
teaspoon
wooden spoon

scissors
pudding basin
large saucepan or steamer
panstand
greaseproof paper
pudding cloth (optional)
string

METHOD

1    Cut a circle of greaseproof paper the size of the top of the pudding basin.
2    Grease (12) the pudding basin.
3    Put flour, spice, breadcrumbs, suet, dried fruit and sugar into the mixing bowl and stir well together.
4*   Peel (14) the apple and grate (9) it on to the plate. Stir it into the mixture.
5*   Wipe the orange and grate (9) the orange skin thinly on to the plate. Stir it into the mixture.
6    Cut the orange in half and using the lemon squeezer squeeze out the juice. Stir it into the mixture.
7    Crack (17) the egg shell and carefully drop the egg into the basin and beat (25) until frothy.
8    Add the egg, gravy browning and half the milk to the mixture.
9*   Stir well, adding more milk if required, to make a runny mixture.
10   Carefully pour the mixture into the greased pudding basin.
11   Place circle of greaseproof paper on top of the mixture.
12*  Cover with a double layer of greaseproof paper or pudding cloth and tie with string.

This pudding may be cooked by boiling in a large saucepan in which the water should be half way up the basin – topping up with boiling water as required, or steamed in a steamer in which the base must be kept full of boiling water.

The initial cooking should be for 3 hours. After this the pudding will keep until required, when a further 3 hour cooking is necessary.

# Fruit crumble

FRUIT

200 g (8 oz) fruit (apples, plums, rhubarb, gooseberries OR blackcurrants)
50 g (2 oz) sugar (use less for sweet fruit)
1 tbs water

CRUMBLE

75 g (3 oz) flour
40 g (1½ oz) margarine
40 g (1½ oz) sugar

THE FOLLOWING ARE ALSO NEEDED

| | | |
|---|---|---|
| scales | knife | oven cloth |
| mixing bowl | potato peeler (for apples) | baking sheet |
| plate | tablespoon | pie dish |
| | skewer | |
| | scissors (for gooseberries) | |

OVEN TEMPERATURE

Gas mark 4. Electric 180°C (350°F)

METHOD

1    Prepare (14–16) the fruit according to type.
2    Put the fruit into the pie dish and add the water.
3    Sprinkle the 'fruit' sugar over the fruit.
4    Put the flour and margarine into the mixing bowl and add the margarine cut into small pieces.
5*   With the finger tips rub (28) the margarine into the flour until it looks like fine breadcrumbs. Shake the bowl gently to make certain that there are no lumps of fat.
6    Stir in the 'crumble' sugar.
7    Sprinkle the crumble mixture over the fruit and press down lightly with your fingers.
8    Put the pie dish on to the baking sheet.
9*   Bake in the oven for about 30 minutes until the top is golden brown.
10   Test the fruit with the skewer. Hard fruit will take longer than soft fruit. If the fruit is not cooked after half an hour lower the oven heat to mark 2 or 150°C (300°F).

## Melting moment biscuits (*10 biscuits*)

50 g (2 oz) margarine
50 g (2 oz) castor sugar
1 egg (only half required)

75 g (3 oz) self raising flour
15 g ($\frac{1}{2}$ oz) crushed cornflakes
3 glacé cherries

THE FOLLOWING ARE ALSO NEEDED

| | | | |
|---|---|---|---|
| scales | rolling pin | knife | oven cloth |
| mixing bowl | greaseproof paper | fork | baking sheet |
| 2 small basins | | tablespoon | cooling tray |
| plate | | wooden spoon | |
| flour dredger | | fish slice | |

OVEN TEMPERATURE

Gas mark 4. Electric 180°C (350°F)

METHOD

1  Grease (12) the baking sheet.

2  Cut the cherries into quarters.

3*  Put the cornflakes into the centre of the greaseproof paper and crush with the rolling pin.

4  Crack (17) the egg shell and carefully drop the egg into basin and beat (25) with the fork.

5*  Carefully pour half the egg into the second basin and put to one side.

6  Cream (39) the margarine and sugar together until light and fluffy.

7*  Add a teaspoon of egg at a time to the creamed mixture, beating well between each spoonful.

8  Fold (40) in the flour a spoonful at a time.

9*  Turn the dough on to the floured table and knead (29) lightly to form a non-sticky dough (51).

10  On the table roll the dough into a long sausage with your fingers and divide it into 10 pieces.

11*  Roll each piece of dough into a ball with the palm of your hands and then roll in the crushed cornflakes.

12*  Flatten slightly and space on the baking sheet. Put a piece of cherry on the top of each.

13  Bake 15–20 minutes until firm and golden brown.

14  Use a fish slice to lift the melting moments from the baking sheet to the cooling tray.

VARIATIONS

**Chocolate melting moments**: replace 2 tsp of the flour with 2 tsp of cocoa
**Ginger melting moments**: add 1 tsp ground ginger to flour before mixing with other ingredients.

## Milk mould

| | | |
|---|---|---|
| 250 ml (½ pt) milk | FLAVOURINGS | ¼ tsp vanilla essence |
| 1 tbs (rounded) cornflour | OR | 2 tsp coffee essence |
| 1 tbs sugar | OR | 1 tbs cocoa |

THE FOLLOWING ARE ALSO NEEDED

| | | |
|---|---|---|
| basin | tablespoon | mould |
| measuring jug | teaspoon | saucepan |
| | wooden spoon | panstand |
| | | serving plate |

METHOD

1 Fill the mould with cold water and stand to one side.

2 Put the cornflour and the sugar into the basin. For chocolate mould add the cocoa.

3 Add 3 tbs milk and mix to a smooth thin paste. For vanilla and coffee moulds add the essence now. Stir.

4 Heat the remaining milk in the saucepan until boiling, watching all the time.

5 Pour the boiling milk into the basin stirring well with the wooden spoon.

6* Return the cornflour mixture to the saucepan and cook over a low heat, stirring (27) all the time. Continue to boil for 2 minutes until the mixture is thick and smooth.

7 Carefully pour water from the mould, but leave it damp.

8* Pour cornflour mixture into the wet mould and leave to set – approximately 1½ to 2 hours.

9 When the mould is set loosen it gently round the edges.

10 Damp the serving plate slightly.

11* Place the serving plate on top of the mould and carefully turn both over. If necessary shake gently to help the mould to slide on to the middle of the plate.

# Cheese pudding

250 ml (½ pt) milk
50 g (2 oz) white breadcrumbs
15 g (½ oz) margarine
50 g (2 oz) hard cheese

1 egg
large pinch salt
shake of pepper
¼ tsp dry mustard (optional)

THE FOLLOWING ARE ALSO NEEDED

| | | |
|---|---|---|
| scales | knife | pie dish |
| basin | fork | saucepan |
| 2 plates | tablespoon | panstand |
| grater | teaspoon | |
| egg whisk | small cutter | |

OVEN TEMPERATURES
Gas mark 4. Electric 180°C (350°F)

METHOD

1    Heat the milk in the saucepan and remove from the cooker.
2    Add the breadcrumbs, margarine and seasonings. Cover the saucepan and leave to stand for ½ an hour.
3    Grate (9) the cheese on to a plate.
4    Grease (12) the pie dish.
5*   Crack the egg on to a plate and using the cutter separate (18) the yolk from the white by pouring the white into the basin.
6    Whisk (32) the white until stiff.
7    Slip the yolk into the mixture in the saucepan and mix thoroughly.
8    Add the grated cheese to the saucepan and mix thoroughly.
9    Fold (40) the white into the cheese mixture.
10*  Pour the mixture into the pie dish.
11   Bake for 30–40 minutes until well risen and golden brown.
12   Serve immediately.

# Fruit fool

PURÉE
400 g (1 lb) fresh fruit with strong flavour
4 tbs water with juicy fruit OR
8 tbs water with firm fruit
2–3 tbs sugar

CUSTARD
250 ml (½ pt) milk
2 tbs custard powder
1 tbs sugar

THE FOLLOWING ARE ALSO NEEDED

| scales | knife | saucepan |
| mixing bowl | tablespoon | panstand |
| basin | wooden spoon | serving dish OR dishes |
| measuring jug | | |
| sieve | | |
| chopping board | | |

METHOD

1   Prepare the fruit according to type.
2*  Put all the ingredients for the purée into the saucepan over a low heat.
3*  Simmer, stirring (27) often, until the mixture is pulpy.
4*  Sieve (19) the pulp into the mixing bowl. Rinse the saucepan in cold water.
5   In the basin mix the custard powder, sugar and 3 tbs cold milk to a smooth paste.
6   Bring the rest of the milk to the boil in the saucepan.
7   Carefully pour the boiling milk into the basin stirring all the time.
8   Return the custard to the saucepan and reboil, stirring (27) all the time until the mixture thickens – about 1 minute.
9   Pour the hot custard into the purée and mix together thoroughly.
10  Serve in a fruit bowl or individual dishes.

## Macaroni cheese

| | | |
|---|---|---|
| 250 ml ($\frac{1}{2}$ pt) milk | 25 g (1 oz) flour | 2 tsp salt |
| 75 g (3 oz) cheese | 75 g (3 oz) macaroni | small pinch salt |
| 25 g (1 oz) margarine | | shake of pepper |

THE FOLLOWING ARE ALSO NEEDED

| | | | |
|---|---|---|---|
| scales | strainer | wooden spoon | pie dish |
| basin | grater | skewer | 2 saucepans |
| 2 plates | tablespoon | oven cloth | panstand |
| measuring jug | teaspoon | baking sheet | |

OVEN TEMPERATURE

Gas mark 6. Electric 200°C (400°F)

NOTE  The final cooking may be done under the grill if the cheese mixture is still hot.

METHOD

1   Half fill a saucepan with water and bring to the boil.

2*  Remove the saucepan from the heat, and using a tablespoon carefully put the macaroni into the water. Add 2 tsp salt.

3   Return the saucepan to the heat and allow the macaroni to simmer until cooked. Test with the skewer after approximately 7 minutes. The macaroni should be tender but not too soft.

4   Grate (9) the cheese on to a plate.

5   Melt the margarine in the other saucepan and then remove from the heat.

6*  Stir in the flour, using the wooden spoon, until thoroughly mixed.

7   Using the teaspoon, gradually add half the milk, stirring between each spoonful with the wooden spoon.

8   Pour in the rest of the milk and stir carefully.

9   Bring this sauce to the boil, stirring (27) all the time.

10  Still stirring, allow the sauce to boil very gently for 3 minutes until it is thick and creamy.

11  Remove the saucepan from the heat and add $\frac{3}{4}$ of the cheese, salt and pepper.

12  Strain (24) the macaroni when cooked, using the strainer.

13* Carefully stir the melting cheese in the sauce and add the macaroni. Mix thoroughly.

14  Grease (12) the pie dish with a margarine paper.

15* Pour the macaroni mixture carefully in the pie dish. Sprinkle remaining grated cheese over the top.

16  Stand the pie dish on the baking sheet and put into the oven. Bake until the cheese has melted and is brown.

If the pupil is taking this dish home stage 16 may be left until it is required for eating.

## Tea bread

| | |
|---|---|
| 150 g (6 oz) flour | 50 g (2 oz) sugar |
| small pinch salt | 1 tbs golden syrup |
| ½ tsp bicarbonate of soda | 1 egg |
| 40 g (1½ oz) margarine | 3 tbs water |

THE FOLLOWING ARE ALSO NEEDED

| | | |
|---|---|---|
| scales | knife | oven cloth |
| mixing bowl | fork | bread tin |
| basin | tablespoon | cooling tray |
| sieve | teaspoon | panstand |
| | wooden spoon | greaseproof paper |
| | skewer | |

OVEN TEMPERATURE

Gas mark 4. Electric 180°C (350°F)

METHOD

1    Cut a piece of greaseproof paper the size of the bottom of the tin. Grease the bread tin and paper. Then put the paper in the bottom of the tin.

2    Crack (17) the egg shell and carefully drop the egg into the basin and beat (25) with the fork.

3    Sieve (20) the flour, salt and bicarbonate of soda into the mixing bowl and add the margarine cut into small pieces.

4    With the finger tips rub (28) the margarine into the flour until it looks like fine breadcrumbs. Shake the bowl gently to make certain there are no lumps of fat.

5    Stir in the sugar.

6    Make a well in the middle of the mixture and put in the syrup and egg.

7    Put the 3 tbs water into the eggy basin.

8    Gently stir the egg and syrup into the flour mixture. Add enough water from the basin to make a dropping (48) consistency.

9    Put the mixture into the tin and bake for about 40 minutes. Test with the skewer which should come out clean.

10    Turn out on to the cooling tray

11    Serve sliced and buttered.

## Yeast dough

200 g (8 oz) plain flour      125 ml ($\frac{1}{4}$ pt) warm water
1 level tsp salt      15 g ($\frac{1}{2}$ oz) fresh yeast OR 1$\frac{1}{2}$ tsp dried yeast
1 level tsp sugar

THE FOLLOWING ARE ALSO NEEDED
scales          measuring jug      knife
mixing bowl    flour dredger      teaspoon
basin
plate

METHOD
**1**\* Put the flour and salt into the mixing bowl and leave in a warm place. This may be on the radiator, over a saucepan of water, or in a cool oven etc
**2** Prepare the yeast:
FRESH:\* cream the yeast and sugar in the basin with the teaspoon until liquid. Stir in the warm water.
DRIED:\* put the sugar into the warm water in the measuring jug and sprinkle the yeast on top. Stir well and leave until frothy on top – approximately 4 minutes.
**3** Mix warmed flour and make a well in the centre with your hand.
**4** Pour the yeast liquid into the well. Put a little warm water into the yeasty basin or jug.
**5**\* Use your hand to work the flour into the liquid until a soft (49) sticky dough is formed. Add a little of the extra water if required.
**6**\* Beat the dough well with your hand until it no longer sticks to the bowl or your fingers. Turn on to a floured table.
**7**\* Using the fingers of both hands knead (31) the dough for 10 minutes to make it smooth.

## White bread (*Quick method*)

200 g (8 oz) yeast dough

THE FOLLOWING ARE ALSO NEEDED
oven cloth       greased bread tin       cooling tray

OVEN TEMPERATURE
Gas mark 8. Electric 230°C (450°F)

METHOD
1   Follow the directions 1–7 for yeast dough and then:
8*  Shape the dough roughly to fit the tin and place it with the smooth side on top. Press gently into the corners.
9*  Cover with a clean cloth or polythene and put the tin in a warm place for approximately 15–30 minutes until the dough has doubled in size.
10  When the dough has risen put the tin into the oven and bake for 20–30 minutes until brown. Reduce the heat to Mark 4 or 180°C (350°F) and bake for a further 10–15 minutes.
11  When cooked the bread will be crisp and firm and sound hollow when tapped underneath.
12  Cool on the cooling tray.


## Bread rolls

200 g (8 oz) yeast dough

THE FOLLOWING ARE ALSO NEEDED
oven cloth       greased baking sheet       cooling tray

OVEN TEMPERATURE
Gas mark 8. Electric 230°C (450°F)

METHOD
1   Follow the directions 1–7 for yeast dough, and then:
8*  Cut the dough into 8 even sized pieces. Knead (31) each piece until round in shape and smooth underneath.
9*  With the smooth side up, space the rolls evenly on the greased baking sheet.
10* Allow the dough to rise by leaving it to prove in a warm place. When ready the rolls will have doubled in size.
11* Bake the rolls for 10–15 minutes. When cooked the rolls will be golden brown and sound hollow when tapped underneath.

# Queen of puddings

PUDDING

250 ml (½ pt) milk  
50 g (2 oz) white breadcrumbs  
15 g (½ oz) margarine  
2 tsp sugar

1 egg yolk  
few drops of lemon essence  
1 tbs soft jam

MERINGUE  
1 egg white  
25 g (1 oz) castor sugar

THE FOLLOWING ARE ALSO NEEDED

| | | |
|---|---|---|
| scales | knife | baking sheet |
| mixing bowl | fork | greased pie dish |
| basin | tablespoon | saucepan |
| plate | teaspoon | panstand |
| grater | cutter | |
| egg whisk | | |

OVEN TEMPERATURES  
PUDDING: Gas mark 3. Electric 160°C (325°F)  
MERINGUE: Gas mark 2. Electric 150°C (300°F)

METHOD

1   Heat the milk in the saucepan to boiling point and then remove from the cooker.

2   Add breadcrumbs, sugar, lemon essence and margarine to the saucepan. Cover and leave for 15 minutes.

3*  Crack the egg on to the plate and using the cutter separate (18) the yolk from the white by pouring the white into the basin.

4   Slip the yolk into the mixture in the saucepan and mix thoroughly.

5   Put this mixture into the pie dish.

6   Place the pie dish on the baking sheet and bake for 20–30 minutes until set. Then lower the oven heat.

7*  Whisk (32) the egg white stiffly and carefully fold (40) in the castor sugar to to make the meringue.

8*  When the pudding is cooked and still hot carefully spread the jam over the top. Pile the meringue evenly on to the pudding so that the jam is completely covered.

9   Return the pudding to the cooler oven for about ½ hour until the meringue is pale fawn.

**Jam buns** *(8 buns)*

100 g (4 oz) self raising flour     50 g (2 oz) margarine     1 egg (only half required)
pinch of salt                                   50 g (2 oz) sugar              1 tbs jam

THE FOLLOWING ARE ALSO NEEDED

| scales | 2 plates | fork | oven cloth |
|--------|----------|------|------------|
| mixing bowl | flour dredger | wooden spoon | greased baking sheet |
| 2 small basins | knife | fish slice | cooling tray |

OVEN TEMPERATURE
Gas mark 6. Electric 200°C (400°F)

METHOD

1* Put the flour and salt into the mixing bowl and add the margarine cut into small pieces.

2* With the finger tips rub (28) the margarine into the flour until it looks like fine breadcrumbs. Shake the bowl gently to make certain there are no lumps of fat.

3 Add the sugar and mix with the wooden spoon.

4* Crack (17) the egg shell and carefully drop the egg into one small basin and beat (25) with the fork.

5 Carefully pour half the egg into the second small basin and put to one side.

6* Make a well in the centre of the flour mixture and pour in the half egg.

7 Mix with the wooden spoon until the mixture makes a non-sticky dough (51)

8* With the back of the knife scrape the mixture from the wooden spoon back into the bowl.

9 Using your fingers lightly knead (29) the mixture to remove the cracks.

10 Turn on to a floured table and continue to knead (29) until the under side of the dough is smooth.

11* Using your fingers roll the mixture into a long sausage shape until it is about 8 in. long.

12 Divide the sausage shape into 8 pieces, starting in the middle.

13* Roll each piece into a round ball and flatten slightly between your hands.

14 Use the handle of the wooden spoon to make a hole half way through the dough in the centre of each bun.

15* Take a little jam on the tip of the teaspoon and ease it into the hole with the tip of your finger. Do not use too much jam or it will boil out and burn.

16 Seal the jam in the buns by closing the dough over the hole.

17* Place the buns on the greased baking sheet with the sealed side down as far apart as possible.

18 Bake in the oven for 15–20 minutes until golden brown.

19 Test with the skewer, which should come out clean.

20 Using a fish slice lift the buns on to the cooling tray.

**Rock cakes** *(8 cakes)*

| | |
|---|---|
| 100 g (4 oz) self raising flour | 1 medium egg (only half required) |
| 50 g (2 oz) margarine | 50 g (2 oz) dried fruit |
| 50 g (2 oz) sugar | 2 tbs milk |
| small pinch salt | |

THE FOLLOWING ARE ALSO NEEDED

| | | |
|---|---|---|
| scales | knife | oven cloth |
| mixing bowl | fork | greased baking sheet |
| 2 small basins | teaspoon | cooling tray |
| measuring jug | wooden spoon | serving plate |
| sieve | fish slice | |
| | skewer | |

OVEN TEMPERATURE
Gas mark 6. Electric 200°C (400°F)

METHOD

1    Crack (17) the egg shell and carefully drop the egg into one small basin and beat (25) with the fork.

2    Carefully pour half the egg into the second small basin and put to one side.

3    Sieve (20) the flour and salt into the mixing bowl and add the margarine cut into small pieces.

4*    With the finger tips rub (28) the margarine into the flour until it looks like fine breadcrumbs. Shake the bowl gently to make certain there are no lumps of fat.

5    Add the sugar and dried fruit to the rubbed-in mixture and mix with the wooden spoon.

6    Add the half egg to the mixture and stir.

7    Then add a teaspoon of milk at a time and stir until a stiff (50) consistency is reached.

8    Using the teaspoon and fork put the mixture on to the baking sheet in even-sized heaps leaving a space between each one.

9    Bake in the oven for 12 to 15 minutes.

10    Using the fish slice lift the cakes on to the cooling tray.

## Fresh fruit salad

1 red eating apple (if not red skinned, apple is better peeled)
1 banana     1 orange
Other fresh fruit can be added according to season
125 ml ($\frac{1}{4}$ pt) water     3 tbs sugar

THE FOLLOWING ARE ALSO NEEDED

| | | |
|---|---|---|
| mixing bowl | vegetable knife | saucepan |
| measuring jug | potato peeler | panstand |
| strainer | tablespoon | serving dish OR dishes |
| chopping board | wooden spoon | |
| paper towel | | |

METHOD

1* Peel (14) the orange very thinly using the potato peeler.

2 Put the orange peel, water and sugar into the saucepan. Bring the water slowly to the boil, stirring all the time, to help dissolve the sugar. Leave this syrup to cool.

3* Wash the apple and dry with a paper towel. Cut (16) in half, then quarters and take out the core. Then cut each piece into thin slices, and put in the mixing bowl.

4 Carefully strain the syrup over the apples in the bowl.

5 Peel the banana and slice into thin rings. Add to the mixing bowl.

6* Using the point of the knife carefully remove the white pith from the orange.

7 Using your thumb break the orange in half along the segments and remove the centre core.

8* Lay the flat side of the orange on to the chopping board and cut (15) slices across the flesh. Add flesh and juice to the mixing bowl.

9 Mix the fruit and liquid together with the wooden spoon. This fruit salad can either be served in a large bowl or individual dishes.

**Victoria sandwich** (*One stage method*)

| | |
|---|---|
| 100 g (4 oz) self raising flour | 100 g (4 oz) castor sugar |
| small pinch salt | 2 eggs |
| 1 tsp baking powder | Filling 1 tbs jam |
| 100 g (4 oz) soft margarine | Decoration icing OR castor sugar |

THE FOLLOWING ARE ALSO NEEDED

| | | |
|---|---|---|
| scales | knife | oven cloth |
| mixing bowl | teaspoon | 2 sandwich tins |
| sieve | wooden spoon | cooling tray |
| | skewer | serving plate |

OVEN TEMPERATURE
Gas mark 4. Electric 180°C (350°F)

METHOD

1 Grease the sandwich tins and lightly sprinkle with flour.

2 Place all the ingredients in the mixing bowl.

3* Beat (26) with the wooden spoon until smooth – approximately 2–3 minutes.

4* Divide the mixture between the 2 tins and smooth flat (41) with the knife. Do not get the mixture on to the sides of the tin or it will burn.

5* Bake for 25–35 minutes. Test the cake by pressing the centre gently with a finger. The mark formed should spring back immediately leaving no dent. Young children may find it easier to use a skewer.

6 Cool on the cooling tray.

7 Sandwich the 2 cakes together with jam.

8* Sieve (20) icing or castor sugar over the top.

## Victoria sandwich (*Creaming method*)

| | |
|---|---|
| 100 g (4 oz) self raising flour | Filling – butter cream: |
| small pinch salt | 50 g (2 oz) icing sugar |
| 100 g (4 oz) margarine | 50 g (2 oz) butter OR margarine |
| 100 g (4 oz) castor sugar | Decoration: |
| 2 eggs | icing OR castor sugar |

THE FOLLOWING ARE ALSO NEEDED

| | | |
|---|---|---|
| scales | knife | oven cloth |
| mixing bowl | fork | 2 sandwich tins |
| basin | 2 tablespoons | cooling tray |
| plate | wooden spoon | serving plate |
| sieve | skewer | |

OVEN TEMPERATURE
Gas mark 4. Electric 180°C (350°F)

METHOD

1    Grease the sandwich tins and lightly sprinkle with flour.

2*   Put the margarine and sugar into the mixing bowl and cream (39) them with the wooden spoon until the mixture turns paler in colour and looks fluffy. If the margarine is very hard it will help to soften it slightly if the mixing bowl is put into a bowl of hot water or stood on a radiator.

3    Crack (17) the egg shell and carefully drop the egg into the basin and beat (25) well with the fork.

4    Sieve (20) the flour and salt on to the plate.

5*   Add a spoonful of egg and a spoonful of flour to the creamed mixture and beat thoroughly.

6    Add the rest of the egg a spoonful at a time and beat very thoroughly after each spoonful.

7    Fold (40) in the rest of the flour as gently as possible, to make the mixture smooth.

8*   Divide the mixture between the 2 tins and smooth flat (41) with the knife. Do not get the mixture on the sides of the tin or it will burn.

9*   Bake for about 15–25 minutes. Test the cake by pressing the centre gently with a finger. The mark formed should spring back immediately leaving no dent. Young children may find it easier to use a skewer.

10   Cool on a cooling tray.

11   Sandwich together with the butter cream.

12*  Sieve (20) icing or castor sugar over the top or cover with icing.

BUTTER CREAM
1   Cream (39) together the fat and sugar until light and fluffy.
2   Add flavouring to taste.

WATER ICING
1   Sieve (20) 4 heaped tbs of icing sugar into a bowl or basin.
2   Add 2 tsp of water to the bowl and stir with the wooden spoon. If the mixture is too stiff, add extra water a DROP at a time until a soft mixture is formed. The icing should spread easily with a knife without running off the edge of the cake.

VARIATIONS IN FLAVOURING
**Chocolate:** omit 1 level tbs of flour and sieve 1 tbs of cocoa with the remaining flour.

Chocolate butter cream can be made by making a paste of 1 tsp of cocoa with 1 tsp of hot water and adding it to the creamed fat and sugar.

**Orange** OR **Lemon:** add the finely grated rind of $\frac{1}{2}$ an orange or lemon at Stage 2:

The other half of the finely grated rind can be used in the butter cream.

The juice can be used in the water icing in place of the water.

**Coffee:** dissolve 1 heaped tsp of instant coffee powder with 2 tsp of hot water and add at stage 6.

Coffee butter cream can be made by making a paste of 1 tsp of coffee powder with 1 tsp of hot water and adding it to the creamed fat and sugar.

# Queen cakes (*12 cakes*)

100 g (4 oz) self raising flour     50 g (2 oz) castor sugar
small pinch salt     1–2 tbs milk
50 g (2 oz) margarine     1 egg
25 g (1 oz) dried fruit (sultanas, currants, cherries, etc)

THE FOLLOWING ARE ALSO NEEDED

| scales | knife | oven cloth |
|---|---|---|
| mixing bowl | fork | bun tin |
| basin | tablespoon | cooling tray |
| plate | teaspoon | serving plate |
| sieve | wooden spoon | paper cases |

OVEN TEMPERATURE
Gas mark 5. Electric 190°C (375°F)

METHOD

1   Grease the bun tin or line with paper cases.

2   Following the directions 2–7 for the creaming method given under Victoria Sandwich, page 86.

8*   Then add enough milk to make a dropping (48) consistency.

9   Stir in the dried fruit.

10   Using the teaspoon, carefully put the mixture into the paper cases (42). Do not over fill.

11*   Bake for 12–15 minutes. Test with the finger by pressing on cake gently in the middle.

12   Cool on the cooling tray.

## Gingerbread

200 g (8 oz) plain flour
1 tsp bicarbonate of soda
1 tsp ground ginger
50 g (2 oz) brown sugar

150 g (6 oz) black treacle
100 g (4 oz) margarine
1 egg
60 ml ($\frac{1}{8}$ pt) milk

THE FOLLOWING ARE ALSO NEEDED

| | | |
|---|---|---|
| scales | knife | oven cloth |
| mixing bowl | fork | square tin 18 cm (7 in.) |
| basin | tablespoon | cooling tray |
| plate | teaspoon | saucepan |
| measuring jug | wooden spoon | panstand |
| sieve | | serving plate |
| | | greaseproof paper |

NOTE: The imperial quantity will be too large for an 18 cm tin, therefore if a slightly larger tin is not available, use paper cases to make several small cakes.

OVEN TEMPERATURE
Gas mark 3. Electric 160°C (325°F)

METHOD

1  Cut out a piece of greaseproof paper to fit the bottom of the tin. Grease (12) this and the sides of the tin with the margarine paper.

2*  Put the margarine, sugar and syrup into the small saucepan. Heat gently, stirring until the margarine has just melted. Do NOT boil. Leave to cool until you can bear your hand on the side of the saucepan.

3  Sieve (20) the dry ingredients into the mixing bowl and make a well in the centre.

4  Crack (17) the egg shell and carefully drop the egg into the basin and beat (25) thoroughly.

5  Pour the cooled melted mixture from the saucepan into the centre of the mixing bowl, together with the beaten egg, and stir well.

6  Add enough milk to make a smooth thick batter (47).

7  Pour carefully into the prepared tin.

8  Bake for $\frac{3}{4}$–1 hour until the cake has shrunk away from the sides of the tin and is firm to the touch.

9  Cool on a cooling tray.

# Scones

| | |
|---|---|
| 100 g (4 oz) self raising flour | ½ tsp baking powder |
| large pinch salt | 60 ml (⅛ pt) milk for mixing |
| 25 g (1 oz) margarine | 2 tsp milk for glazing |

THE FOLLOWING ARE ALSO NEEDED

| | | | |
|---|---|---|---|
| scales | knife (round bladed) | skewer | oven cloth |
| mixing bowl | tablespoon | pastry brush | baking sheet |
| measuring jug | teaspoon | | cooling tray |
| flour dredger | wooden spoon | | |

OVEN TEMPERATURE
Gas mark 8. Electric 230°C (450°F)

METHOD

1 Grease (12) the baking sheet with the margarine paper.

2* Put the flour and salt into the mixing bowl and add the margarine cut into small pieces.

3* With the finger tips rub (28) the margarine into the flour until it looks like fine breadcrumbs. Shake the bowl gently to make certain there are no lumps of fat.

4* Add all the 'mixing milk' and mix quickly with the wooden spoon or knife to form a soft dough (49).

5* Turn the dough on to a lightly floured table and knead (29) lightly until it is smooth and round.

6* With the smoothest side on top gently flatten the dough with the palm of your hand until it is 2 cm (¾ in.) thick.

7* With the knife make 2 cuts through the centre of the dough to form a deep cross. The four scones formed can easily be broken apart when cooked.

8 Place the scones on to the baking sheet and brush (44) the top with milk.

9 Bake for 10–15 minutes, until well risen and brown on top.

10 Cool on a cooling tray.

When a cutter is used as many scones as possible should be cut the first time. Then the remaining dough should be re-kneaded before cutting again.

VARIATIONS
**Sweet scones:** add 1 tbs of sugar after stage 3 and mix together.
**Currant scones:** add 1 tbs of sugar and 1 tbs of currants after stage 3, and mix together.
**Cheese scones:** add 2 rounded tbs of grated cheese after stage 3 and mix together.

## Short crust pastry

| | |
|---|---|
| 100 g (4 oz) plain flour | large pinch salt |
| 50 g (2 oz) fat (half white, half margarine) | 1–2 tbs cold water |

THE FOLLOWING ARE ALSO NEEDED

| | | |
|---|---|---|
| scales | plate | knife (round bladed) |
| mixing bowl | flour dredger | tablespoon |
| small basin | rolling pin | teaspoon |

METHOD

1  Put the flour and the salt into the mixing bowl and add the fat cut into small pieces.

2  With the finger tips rub (28) the fat into the flour until it looks like fine breadcrumbs. Shake the bowl gently to make certain there are no lumps of fat.

3*  Sprinkle 1 tbs water over this mixture and bind together using the knife. If the dough does not stick together add more water, a teaspoon at a time, until it does. The dough should hold together without being sticky (51).

4  Turn the dough on to a lightly floured table.

5*  Knead (29) lightly until the dough is smooth and round.

6  With the smoothest side on top roll (30) the pastry with a floured rolling pin. Do not turn the pastry over.

## Open tart

| | |
|---|---|
| 100 g (4 oz) short crust pastry | 2 tbs jam |

THE FOLLOWING ARE ALSO NEEDED
oven cloth       ovenproof plate

OVEN TEMPERATURE
Gas mark 6. Electric 200°C (400°F)

METHOD

1  Make the pastry as described in the previous recipe.

2  Roll (30) the pastry until approximately 3 mm ($\frac{1}{8}$ in.) thick, and slightly larger than the plate.

3*  Fold the pastry in half and lift on to the plate. Unfold the pastry and carefully line the plate. Do not stretch.

4*  Lift the plate on to the palm of your left hand and trim the edge of the pastry with the knife by cutting against the side of the plate.

5  Using the handle of the tablespoon decorate the edge of the tart.

6  Spoon the jam into the centre of the plate and spread outwards. Put enough jam, but not so much that it will boil over.

7  Bake the tart for 15–20 minutes until the pastry is golden brown.

# Apple pie

150 g (6 oz) short crust pastry    Glaze:
600 g (1½ lb) apples      1 tsp water
50 g (2 oz) sugar      ½ tsp sugar

THE FOLLOWING ARE ALSO NEEDED

| | |
|---|---|
| vegetable knife | oven cloth |
| potato peeler | baking sheet |
| skewer | pie dish |
| pastry brush | pie funnel OR egg cup |

OVEN TEMPERATURE
Gas mark 7. Electric 220°C (425°F)

METHOD

1 Make the short crust pastry.
2 Roll (30) the pastry out to the shape of the pie dish, but larger, as shown in the photograph.
3* Follow the photographs 33 and 34 for cutting the pastry top and strips.
4 Prepare the apples by peeling, coring and slicing (16).
5 Place a funnel in the centre of the pie dish. This may be an upturned egg cup.
6* Put the apples into the pie dish in layers round the funnel with the sugar sprinkled in between. Pile the apple in the centre to just above the level of the pie dish.
7* Damp (35) the rim of the pie dish with water. Lay the pastry strips on to the rim and press the joins lightly together. Damp the strips.
8 Cover, decorate and glaze the pie following photographs 36 to 38 and 43.
9* Put the pie dish on to the baking sheet and bake for 20 minutes until the pastry is brown. Test the fruit with the skewer through the central cross. If uncooked put the pie on to a lower shelf to finish cooking.

VARIATIONS
The following fruits are also suitable for pies – rhubarb, gooseberries, blackcurrants, blackberries, plums. If the fruits are very sour extra sugar will be needed.

## *Plain omelette

| | |
|---|---|
| 1 large egg | knob of butter |
| pinch of salt | 1 tbs of water |
| shake of pepper | |

THE FOLLOWING ARE ALSO NEEDED

| basin | fork | oven cloth | small omelette pan |
|---|---|---|---|
| | tablespoon | large baking sheet | serving plate |
| | spatula | panstand | |

METHOD

1   Put the serving plate to warm.
2   Crack (17) the egg shell and let the egg slide into the basin.
3   Add the seasonings and water.
4   Beat (25) with the fork until it becomes frothy.
5*  Melt the butter in the omelette pan over medium heat, tilting the pan so that the whole surface is evenly greased. Avoid browning the butter by over-heating.
6*  Carefully pour the egg mixture into the pan. As it sets draw the edge into the middle with the spatula and allow liquid egg to run on to the pan.
7*  Cook for 1–2 minutes until the egg is set and the under-side is lightly browned. Lift the edge of the omelette with the spatula to check browning.
8   When cooked fold the omelette in half.
9   Turn on to the hot serving plate and eat immediately.

FILLINGS

An omelette may be filled after stage 7. The filling should be prepared before cooking the egg and then spread on half the omelette before folding.

**Cheese:** 1 heaped tbs finely grated cheese.
**Herbs:** $\frac{1}{2}$ tsp finely chopped fresh herbs or a pinch of dried herbs.
**Ham:** 1 tbs chopped ham.

## *Pancakes (*8 pancakes*)

100 g (4 oz) plain flour    small pinch salt
1 egg    25 g (1 oz) white fat for frying
250 ml (½ pt) milk

TO SERVE:
2 tbs castor sugar
1 tbs lemon juice

THE FOLLOWING ARE ALSO NEEDED

| scales | measuring jug | fish slice | greaseproof paper |
| mixing bowl | sieve | frying pan | serving plate |
| basin | fork | large baking sheet | |
| plate | wooden spoon | panstand | |

METHOD

1    Sieve (20) the flour and salt into the mixing bowl.

2    Crack (17) the egg shell and let the egg slide into the basin. Beat (25) slightly with fork.

3*    Make a hole in the centre of the flour and pour the egg into it.

4    Pour about half of the milk into the basin and mix with the remains of the egg.

5    Pour this liquid into the hole in the flour.

6*    Using the wooden spoon gradually mix the flour into the liquid working from the centre outwards.

7    When the flour is all mixed, beat (26) the mixture thoroughly until the batter is smooth. Large air bubbles should form in the batter.

8    Stir in the rest of the milk gently.

9    Put the greaseproof paper on to the plate and sprinkle with sugar.

10    Carefully pour the batter into the jug. Put the serving plate to warm.

11*    Heat about 5 g (¼ oz) of fat in the frying pan until very hot. When a blue haze is formed lower the heat.

12*    Gently pour just enough batter into the frying pan to coat the base very thinly, tilting the pan so that it spreads evenly.

13*    Fry gently until the batter is set and the pancake is golden brown underneath.

14*    Turn (45–46) or toss, the pancake very carefully.

15*    Fry the other side until brown.

16    Turn the pancake on to the sugared paper, sprinkle with lemon juice and roll up.

17    Serve and eat immediately.

## Peppermint creams

200 g (8 oz) icing sugar
1 small egg white OR 1½ tbs evaporated milk
10 drops essence of peppermint
3 drops green colouring (optional)

THE FOLLOWING ARE ALSO NEEDED

| | | |
|---|---|---|
| scales | knife (round bladed) | baking sheet |
| mixing bowl | tablespoon | |
| basin | teaspoon | |
| plate | wooden spoon | |
| sieve | small cutter | |
| egg whisk | | |

METHOD

1* Crack the egg shell and let the egg slide on to the plate. Place (18) the cutter round the yolk and let the white drain into the mixing bowl. Put the yolk into the basin. Wash and dry the plate thoroughly.

2 Beat the egg white slightly, and add colouring and flavouring.

3 Sieve (20) the icing sugar on to the plate.

4 Add the icing sugar gradually to the egg white, a tablespoon at a time, until a firm paste is formed.

5 Knead (29) the paste in the mixing bowl until the paste is smooth.

6 Take a small piece of paste and roll to a round ball between the palms of the hands.

7 Place the ball on the baking sheet and flatten with the knife. Leave until set and then loosen from the sheet with the knife.

The paste may be rolled out and cut with fancy cutters.
Be warned – it is a messy operation.

# Index